Piercing the Autumn Sky

With Best
Wishes !

Piercing the Autumn Sky

A Guide to Discovering
the
Natural Freedom
of
Mind

Peter F. Barth

Lame Turtle Press
Petaluma, California

Lame Turtle Press
P.O. Box 750681
Petaluma, CA 94975-0681
USA

9 8 7 6 5 4 3 2 1

First edition

Printed in USA

Cover design by Kurt West

Cover photograph of Dukchen Thuksay Rinpoche taken by author in Darjeeling in autumn of 1974. Dukchen Thuksay Rinpoche was the author's first Mahamudra teacher.

Library of Congress Catalogue Number 93-77066

ISBN 0-9635796-3-0

Publisher's Cataloging in Publication

Barth, Peter F.
    Piercing the autumn sky : a guide to discovering the natural freedom of mind / Peter F. Barth.
        p. cm.
    Preassigned LCCN: 93-77066.
    ISBN 0-9635796-3-0

    1. Meditation. 2. Spiritual life (Buddhism). I. Title.

BQ7805.B37 1993   158'.1

Foreword

On the Buddhist Path we believe that to overcome our confusion and suffering, we must look not only outward to our environment, but we must look inward, which is to say, we must look at our mind.

Peter Barth's *Piercing the Autumn Sky* is a clearly written book which lays out how one can work with one's mind to overcome the obstacles in one's life. Peter writes in a clear and concise manner and is to be commended for not slipping into long technical phrases.

Piercing the Autumn Sky covers such important topics as the impermanence of life, the law of karma, and the use of meditation to understand the mind. The book also includes some interesting practical exercises on how to actually grasp some of these concepts.

Kenchen Thrangu Rinpoche

Lake Big Bear, California
Thanksgiving, 1992

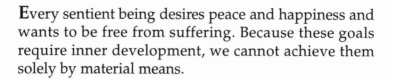

Every sentient being desires peace and happiness and wants to be free from suffering. Because these goals require inner development, we cannot achieve them solely by material means.

How, then, do we attain the necessary mental qualities? Buddha's teachings fully explain that these qualities come only through the study and practice of love, compassion, and wisdom — crucial for the realization of harmonious peace and happiness in both relative and absolute states.

Peter Barth's *Piercing the Autumn Sky* is written in simple language and a clear, accessible style in order to help those on the Dharma path. Easily readable, it draws from the author's own long-term experience with Mahamudra practice. *Piercing the Autumn Sky* will quench the thirst of the spiritual seeker.

From *The Garland of Mahamudra Practices*, this essential passage illustrates the mode of being of all natural phenomena:

> The precious lama (Lord Phagmo Drupa) understood that all migrators wander in cyclic existence because they hold the view of the aggregates as inherently existent — a view that

is false because of mental elaborations. Therefore the lama taught the view free from elaboration; he taught meditation on that view without distraction; and he taught practice of the ethics of the Buddha. These three — pure view, pure meditation, and pure practice — are the supreme essence of the Buddha's teaching.

With prayers and blessings,

Khenpo Könchog Gyaltsen Rinpoche

Frederick, Maryland
January, 1993

Credits

Grateful acknowledgment is made for the permission to reprint excerpts from the following sources:

The Eastern Buddhist, Vol. XIII, No. 2, Autumn 1980, "Zen Master Hakuin's Poison Words for the Heart," translated by Norman Waddell. Copyright © 1980 by Norman Waddell. Used by permission of Norman Waddell. (Hakuin Zenji, p.97.)

A First Zen Reader compiled and translated by Trevor Leggett. Copyright © 1960 by Charles E. Tuttle Co., Inc. Used by permission of Charles E. Tuttle Co., Inc. of Tokyo, Japan. (Hakuin Zenji, p.92.)

The Garland of Mahamudra Practices by Kunga Rinchen, translated and introduced by Khenpo Rinpochay Könchog Gyaltsen, co-translated and edited by Katherine Rogers. Copyright © 1986 by Khenpo Rinpochay Könchog Gyaltsen and Katherine Rogers. Used by permission of Snow Lion Publications, Ithaca, NY.

Mahamudra: The Quintessence of Mind and Meditation by Takpo Tashi Namgyal, translated by Lobsang P. Lhalungpa. Copyright © 1986 by Lobsang P. Lhalungpa. Used by permission of Shambhala Publications, Inc., Boston, MA. (Bodhicaryavatara.)

Zen Comments on the Mumonkan by Zenkei Shibayama. Copyright © 1974 by Zenkei Shibayama. Used by permission of HarperCollins Publishers. (Japanese Waka Poem, Japanese Haiku Poem, Zen Poem, Mumon, Zen Comment.)

Zen Poems of China and Japan by Lucien Stryk, Takashi Ikemoto and Taigan Takayama. Copyright © 1973 by Lucien Stryk, Takashi Ikemoto and Taigan Takayama. Used by permission of Doubleday, a division of Bantam Doubleday Dell Publishing Group, Inc. (Gizan, Honei, Myotan.)

Contents

Part Three - **Dispelling Confusion From Our Path**

Part Four - **Confusion Arises as Pristine Awareness**

Preface

If one does not know
The secret nature of the mind
Which is the essence of all dharma,
One may wander aimlessly,
Though one wished to
Be happy and eliminate misery.

Bodhicaryavatara

The importance of understanding the nature of mind is something that we are all ready to acknowledge. Our minds are the basis for our lives and our experience. When we happen to feel vibrant and good, the universe is a wonderful place to be; when we happen to feel terrible, the universe is a living hell. Clearly, from an experiential perspective, mind underlies all experience and provides the foundation for the way we view ourselves and the universe.

However, when it comes to developing an understanding of mind, we usually don't know where to begin. Furthermore, if we wish to live within the context of our understanding, we are at an even greater loss. It is easy to acknowledge the importance of understanding the mind on an intellectual level but not so easy to develop that understanding and cultivate our lives with respect to it.

Unfortunately most of us never take up the challenge of exploring our own mind. Or if we take up the challenge, we only go so far with it, barely penetrating the surface. It is the irony of mind that when you ignore it, you tend to have a sense of feeling lost, but if you look for it, even though you are unable to find something tangible, this feeling of "being lost" vanishes. The search itself can bring meaning into our lives, whereas the discovery of the nature of mind has the possibility of bringing us endless fulfillment.

So how can we begin an exploration of who we are?

Of course there are endless possibilities here. We can try to study everything that is known about the mind, perhaps pursuing the psychology and philosophy of mind. This will allow us to develop many interesting theories but, in the end, these theories will probably frustrate us because of their inherent limitations, like artwork which remains unfinished. Regardless of how wonderful a model might be, we cannot even be sure that the assumptions upon which it is based are correct. Ultimately, if we apply only this "analytical approach" we will leave this life feeling hollow and dry, having made little genuine progress in understanding mind.

An alternate approach which we may come upon is called the "experiential approach." By looking carefully and sensitively at who we are and directly investigating the nature of our mind and its perceptions and thoughts, we have the possibility of developing some fresh and highly relevant understanding.

Unfortunately, our culture lacks a systematic approach for experientially investigating the nature of mind. Also, if we look around at other cultures on our planet, we may remain unclear as to what they have to offer in this regard. Even if we discover something of value, we do not know how to proceed; the cultural gaps seem too large to overcome.

It is only in recent years that one of the world's ancient cultures has made its vast body of teachings available to the west. Indeed, within the traditions of the people of Tibet exists a body of knowledge referred to as the "mind teachings." It is here that we find a vast and alive tradition which deals with direct investigations of the nature of mind. It is precisely in the "mind teachings" of the Tibetan Kagyu and Nyingma lineages that a profound, well-tested, and well-defined experiential approach to understanding mind has been maintained explicitly "for the benefit of all sentient beings." As a student and lay practitioner of these teachings for the past twenty years, this is the approach which I introduce in this book. If there is anything of merit here, it originates from the oral teachings and sacred writings of these wonderful people of the Land of Snow.

The mind teachings are regarded as the essence of what is transmitted in the Kagyu and Nyingma lineages of Tibet. They are remarkably unencumbered by cultural forms. In my experience, they do not cause Westerners to feel as if something "foreign" is being imposed on them. Indeed, these teachings speak directly to the heart of anyone who chooses to listen to them.

Readers who are familiar with Tibetan teachings will recognize that the book is divided into four parts in accordance with the four truths of Gampopa, the father of the Kagyu lineages. The discussion herein focuses on what Gampopa referred to as the "path of direct awakening." Both introductory and advanced topics are presented.

The path to awakening to the nature of mind "as it is" is traditionally summarized as consisting of the three stages of listening to, examining, and practicing the teachings, the truth. The real value of these ancient teachings lies in their simplicity and directness. In life, we take many side roads, we look for many diversions. Here we have a direct path which can keep us on track. Indeed, only when we make a sincere commitment to investigating our nature and living in accordance with that nature, are we on a true course.

With all the excellent texts on Tibetan teachings now appearing in the English language, I debated the merit of an additional book. However, for several years it seems that there has been a need for a book which presents the mind teachings of Tibet in a simple and accessible format for Westerners who are totally unfamiliar with Tibetan language and the intricacies of its philosophical frameworks. It is my hope that the present book will serve this purpose in a small way.

Acknowledgments

I wish to acknowledge and express my deep gratitude to the following teachers: Kenchen Thrangu Rinpoche, Khenpo Könchog Gyaltsen Rinpoche, Tarthang Tulku Rinpoche, and Dukchen Thuksay Rinpoche. In particular, I would like to thank Thrangu Rinpoche and Khenpo Könchog Gyaltsen Rinpoche for writing forewords to this book, and for bringing the heart of mahamudra to the United States.

In addition, I would like to thank His Holiness Dudjom Rinpoche, Kalu Rinpoche, Namkhai Norbu Rinpoche, Khamtrul Rinpoche, Togden Rinpoche, Geagen Khyentse, Amila Urgyen Chodron, Geshe Lama Sherab Gyaltsen Amipa, the Nyingma Institute, Katagiri Roshi, and Jakusho Kwong Roshi. Also thanks go to the host of translators, Tibetan and Western, who have helped to open up these teachings for us.

Although I only met them through their writings and through their spiritual descendants, I would like to acknowledge the lion's roar of Sri Bhagavan Patanjali, Padma Karpo, Sri Ramana Maharshi, Shunryu Suzuki, and Carl Rogers.

My thanks to Bruce Hindrichs, Bryan Connell, Donna McLaughlin, Frank Cassirer, Gisela Barth, Mark Steiner, Rosemarie Roth, Yeshe Dorje, and all members of Mahamudra Meditation Center, for being good spiritual friends. In particular, I would like to thank Donna McLaughlin and Ilene Barth for their editorial comments and Clark Johnson for his many helpful suggestions.

Finally, thanks to my family, particularly my wife, Ilene, for putting up with all this!

❀

I would like to dedicate this book with all my heart to my daughters, Holly and Rachel, and to all children throughout time and space.

❀　　❀　　❀

Mind Turns Toward Truth

Precious Human Birth

Exploring the nature of time and space,
As present in our lives,
We may begin to discover the vastness
Of time and space itself,
The vastness of our human awareness.

Reflections of Mind

Now that I come to live!

If we take a moment to reflect on the endless stretches of time before our birth and the endless reaches of time after our death, we can develop some sense of how exceptional the event of our human birth is throughout the play of time. Similarly, if we imagine the vastness of space, out past the limits of our solar system and the known universe, and into the smallest territories of atomic particles, we develop some sense of how rare a human body is throughout the reaches of space. Throughout space and time, we are quite an oddity!

A friend once described an experience he had while serving over in Vietnam. One night, he and his fellow troops struck camp on a site from which they could look out over the neighboring fields. It happened to be quiet that night with no sign of "enemy action." When they awoke to the silence the next day, he and his buddies looked out over the surrounding terrain and noticed it was covered by a sea of flying insects. These insects mirrored the contour of the ground by hovering about twelve inches above anything on it. They were beautiful, gossamer creatures, harmless in nature, and they busily used the day to indulge in the rite of procreation.

The soldiers remained on the site for another night and the next morning was accompanied by an even deeper silence. As they looked out over the fields, they noticed that the blanket of insects had completely vanished. Instead, on the ground lay millions of bodies of these effervescent creatures. It then became evident to them that these insects had a life span of only one day. Under the right conditions, once a year, they would simultaneously emerge from their eggs to enjoy life in all its splendor for just one day!

In some regards our life appears to be extremely unique and effervescent, like a bubble on the surface of the ocean. In other respects it can seem quite enduring and expansive, like the ocean itself.

Let us for a moment consider the fact that we can be aware of events on the order of a tenth of a second.

(Remember how long one second felt, when your kindergarten teacher timed it out for you...clap.........clap; and then there was the minute, sitting in our seats in school, a minute seemed like a small eternity!) If we happen to be fortunate enough to live 65 years, this is equivalent to more than 20,000,000,000 of these moments. From this perspective, a lifetime seems eons long, like that of an ancient Greek god.

It may also be interesting to take a few moments to consider the endowments of this human body and mind. If we reflect on our endowments, we may be surprised to discover how wealthy we really are.

With a bit of good fortune, we were born with all five senses in tact. Someone who has had and then lost the sense of sight will tell you two things. First, it is a treasure beyond conception, which should be cherished and appreciated. Second, without it one begins to realize that all the other senses are also treasures. With no longer placing so much emphasis on sight, one begins to discover the richness of sensation, feeling, sound, smell, and taste.

We do not have to be blind to appreciate what these other senses have to offer. We have the ability to see, hear, smell, taste, feel, think, and remember. With our bodies we are able to walk through the space of our environment. Lifting a cup of tea or water to our lips, the miracle of our life unfolds.

If we take a moment to attend to the space aspect of our experience, we can begin to note how vast our experiential space really is. With no scene just like the one before it, experience after experience arises, endlessly varied. From one perspective we can say we are richly endowed with experiential space after experiential space.

Let us suppose, for a moment, that we could travel throughout "all of space." Instead of spending weekends exploring night clubs, beach coves, or mountain valleys, we could explore other planets. We could explore new civilizations and forms of life. This would certainly be a great source of fascination for us. Similarly, if we could travel throughout time, not at the pace of the wall clock but, let us say, 100,000 years into the future or 100,000 years into the past, we could witness, first hand, historic events and people.

In either of these cases what remains clear is that wherever we go, throughout time and space, we will take ourselves with us. Wherever we go, throughout time and space, we still will abide in the so-called "here and now." We can make all of these journeys with our body or in our imagination, or perhaps even somehow directly with our minds. In any case, however, we remain in the "here and now." And in being here and now, in a very real way, we have not gone anywhere else.

The prospects of travel throughout time and space are fascinating for us all. Still, even if we accomplish them — and we have certainly learned to travel through space more efficiently during this last century — it is clear that we come no closer to self-understanding, no closer to ourselves. And, by being carried away by our imagination or our infatuation with new experiences, we may lose sight of the fact that we are actually richly endowed with space and time, as well as other faculties, at every moment and in every circumstance.

Living in the "here and now," if explored, may prove to not be such a big constraint after all. Exploring the nature of time and space more directly, as present in our lives, we may begin to discover the vastness of time and space itself, the vastness of our human awareness. We may note the sameness of each moment, or each millionth of a moment, in the sense that each "piece" of time or space contains the complete nature of all of time and space. We are endowed with space and time itself in the fabric of our being. What an immeasurable endowment!

In addition, our thinking and recollecting mind is able to store "events" from our past, retrieve them and relate them in endless new ways. Our dreams and identities emerge from this, as do all our values. After some reflection, we may choose to do something of meaning with our lives and discover our human dignity, or for reasons beyond our control, we may wind up on skid row. The possibilities are without end.

Our human life is not only precious because it is extraordinarily rare and unique and because it is quite fragile, but also because it is endowed with immeasurable qualities and possibilities.

The Five Aspects of Mind

Underlying the "set of events" which make up our experience, our identity, there is what we call our "mind." Throughout most of our history, it has been uncustomary to think about or take note of the awareness aspect of mind.

In this area, a simple reflection may open new doors for us. We begin by observing that anytime we ask "Is there an awareness which sees all this?" the answer is yes. Even now, you may make note of your awareness. This clarity, this quality of knowing present in mind, in a sense, is "ever present," since whenever we look for it, "it is there."

And looking "there" for it, it cannot be found as existing in a particular location in space. Neither is it restricted to a moment in time nor to a particular language, culture, neighborhood, race, or age.

Somehow awareness is present as all of these and beyond all of these.

The mind teachings of Tibet commonly refer to five elemental qualities intrinsic to mind. These are simply referred to as the space, fire, wind, earth, and water aspects.

The space aspect of mind may be described as the open, unstained quality of mind. Our mind accommodates everything but remains unscathed even by our conceptions of existence and non-existence. In this regard, our mind is like a vast mirror which reflects endless appearances yet remains as it is.

In addition, our mind has a knowing or clarity or self-illuminating quality to it. This is referred to as the fire aspect. The mind has a seeing quality, an awareness, intrinsic to it. This knowing may take on endless forms, but the essence of knowing illuminates all of mind, without cessation, like the sun.

The unceasing, unimpeded aspect of mind and the endless experiences which arise in it express its dynamic or time quality, which is associated with the element wind. Experience constantly changes and is in a state of flux, flashing forth without limitation. It is like a finger drawing a picture on the surface of water; it arises, appears, and subsides all at once.

The ground for all of this is the element earth. The mind is open and illuminating in its essence, yet unceasingly manifesting due to its dynamic quality. The mind, as the root of all experience in life, including our happiness and deep sorrow, acts as the ground of all possibilities. The mind is the ground of our experienced life.

Finally, there is a quality of continuity to mind, like flowing water. The ground of mind is always empty, illuminated, and dynamic in character. This ever-present basis provides continuity to what we call mind. Throughout the interplay of space, time, and awareness, continuity is present, both in conventional and fundamental ways.

Having this wonderfully endowed human mind, few of us have truly learned to appreciate its role in our lives. However, appreciating mind is not limited to recognizing the space, time, awareness, ground, and continuity aspects of it. Our appreciation can extend to all aspects of our life, even the most "ordinary."

We can begin by working on cherishing life itself. How often has an elder of our community advised us: "Take the time to smell the roses!" or "Seize the day!" This advice from our elders should be honored, even though "smelling the roses" may sound very old-fashioned to us.

Appreciating who and what we are right now can be a basis for beginning to appreciate human life, human mind. This appreciation can extend to and embrace all of our daily life and its aspects. We can begin to appreciate the waves of mind as well as its depths.

We do not have to specify any precondition to our life to be able to begin to extend appreciation to it.

After all, its deeper and pervasive aspects will not be held back by any conditions we place on it. I am "too fat," "too thin," "too old," "too young," "too stupid," "too smart," "too messed-up," "too hungry," "too poor," "too busy," "too important," "worthless," "a failure," "a success with too many responsibilities," "too crazy." With all these words we fail to honor who and what we are right now. And we prevent ourselves from beginning to appreciate life.

Even as a very young child, we recognize the value of life. It seems that every child does. And when life is trampled upon or ignored by our parents, friends, teachers, enemies, heroes, those we love, those we hate, we feel a deep sorrow and react in a variety of ways. However, when someone demonstrates value for life, perhaps by holding us in their arms, we are touched. In the holding of someone in our arms, appreciation for life is right there.

At the heart of daily life we begin to realize the "importance of living," of beginning to "respect life." Not killing, not harming ourselves or others, takes on renewed significance for us.

By remembering, touching, and savoring life, this life, at all times and in all conditions, it begins to blossom around us and in us. Everything is taken care of, everything begins to have meaning, and we can come to know the importance of honoring that which we truly are. The one we are right now.

Let us admire the moon and
    Cherish the flowers—
Thus we should like to live.
Never try to become Buddhas
And ruin our precious life!

                    Japanese Waka Poem

The Lesson of Time

Whatever may be our condition in life,
Impermanence serves to remind us
That we cannot afford to be complacent.

The Impermanence of Our Lives

Time is a most mysterious aspect of our lives. Perhaps it is because space is regarded as consisting of three dimensions (length, width, and height) and time is regarded to be only one dimension (like a one-way street), that we remain more mystified by the nature of time than that of space. Like the inhabitants of *Flatland* trying to understand three-dimensional forms as they float through their two-dimensional world, we can never quite figure it out.

On a conventional level, impermanence is at the core of what we experience about the world. Even if we build the most fantastic fortress-palace to entertain ourselves in and protect ourselves with, as the years go by we will see signs of its aging. And of ours. There is no escaping time.

Impermanence serves to remind us that as long as we identify with "body" or "mind," our physical beauty, our accomplishments, our thoughts, our images, we will remain bewildered. As long as we identify with the waves of mind without regard to its depths, we suffer.

Taking for granted that we are this "body," we never really investigate what body is. Thinking that we know the nature of our "mind," we never seriously investigate it. And then as "body" and "mind" deteriorate, we are terrified.

In our lives, the "flow of time" can appear to be at once both threatening and liberating in character. Time manifests as perpetual change while also ensuring that we will not become stuck anywhere, in any situation, regardless of how unpleasant it is. We have all been "defeated by the clock" as well as "saved by the bell!"

Whatever may be our condition in life, impermanence serves to remind us that we cannot afford to be complacent.

Laziness, idleness, preoccupation with exciting and sensual experiences, addiction to "things we have to do"... the lures of laziness and endless endeavor, like the songs of the sirens on the rocks, call to us. Today in

America we can entertain ourselves from morning to night if we choose; or we can "work our brains out" until we drop dead. Yet the threatening aspect of time is always there to remind us that becoming attached to things, sleep, idleness, hard work, or "entertained states of mind" is of no value and that idleness, sensory diversions, and hard work aimed at "worldly" matters will ultimately not save us from the destruction of change.

We may have a smug sense of hope that somehow we will be saved from time's destructive power, even if we have no clear idea of how. We may call this sense "faith in life" or "faith in God." Or we may cling to depressed or despondent states, hoping that these attitudes will prepare us for the inevitable cataclysms which time will dish out to us.

We may even hope for a breakthrough in science. Perhaps someone will discover a technological elixir of immortality in our lifetime or a means for transferring our consciousness to vehicle after vehicle. Perhaps.

It is helpful to consider precisely how it is that we deal with the fact of endless change in our lives. What is our personal view on this?

In any case, the only thing we can be certain of is the destructive (and creative) power of time itself. Time is always telling us something and we should all listen to its message.

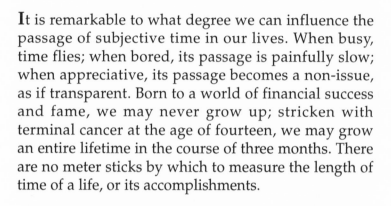

It is remarkable to what degree we can influence the passage of subjective time in our lives. When busy, time flies; when bored, its passage is painfully slow; when appreciative, its passage becomes a non-issue, as if transparent. Born to a world of financial success and fame, we may never grow up; stricken with terminal cancer at the age of fourteen, we may grow an entire lifetime in the course of three months. There are no meter sticks by which to measure the length of time of a life, or its accomplishments.

It is the greatest sorrow when a child dies at an early age. At the same time, who can measure the vastness of even one child's life? A moment can be as vast as a lifetime and contains all the elements and potential of life in it. It also contains all the accomplishments of life, although it may not contain the imaginary ones we may wish upon it or cry out and demand for it.

In an attempt to be clever with respect to time, "get the edge" so-to-speak, we may explore different ways of increasing the longevity of our lives. Pursuing spiritual paths, praying for longevity, changing partners or careers, working out, or eating health foods. Whether we look for longevity by any of these means, the aging process is at best slowed down or only temporarily reversed. Like a finger in a dike, their effects do not last.

Finally, we must come to terms with the dynamic quality of ourselves and our world, of our mind. And in getting to know the time quality of mind, we may discover something of extraordinary value.

Learning to Relate to Time

Eventually we may decide to challenge our preconceptions about the nature of time. Rather than a linear road that we are on, we may discover what may be called vast time, a time which is inherent in everything, as eternal, unimpeded dynamism; a source of unlimited energy.

By getting to know this aspect of our minds, by attending to the dynamic nature of our experience directly, we can actually begin to enter the dance of vast time itself, with no space between "us" and "time." The fabrications of "past," "present," and "future" places and selves begin to loosen their grip on us. Experientially, we realize that the past and future are only projections of our thoughts, while the present remains an indeterminate state that cannot be pinned down.

Appreciating the dynamism of our experience underlying "moment after moment," we begin to discover the self-liberating quality of everything we experience. Completely free, while arising, while subsiding. Appreciation of the time quality of our minds can take us directly beyond the constructs of mind itself to its more timeless aspects.

Attending to the time or space aspects of experience can have an immediately liberating effect on us. This is a simple practice, one which we may incorporate in our daily life and it is at the core of the practice of mindfulness, gentle mindfulness. By simply applying this mindfulness we directly step into time itself, vast time.

The act of remembering time and its message can take place on a gross level for example, when we experience the death of a loved one. Or it can occur at a more subtle level, by attending to the time aspect of all that arises. Ultimately, the very act of "remembering or attending" is self-liberated, completely and naturally, in the dance of time. We discover that we are the dance of time itself. At this stage we no longer have to make an effort to connect with time. Every display of time, even our present condition, is like a ray of sunlight coming from the sun, intimately linked to its source. With nothing to hold back, we have found the secret to eternal life right now in this life.

In physics, there is some interest in what is called the "arrow of time." Some have attempted various ways of differentiating between "backward" and "forward" flowing time. It has been pointed out that spontaneous events in the universe of "forward flowing time" seem to always result in an increase in "entropy" — a measure of disorder in a system — and that it appears that we are all trending towards maximum "loss of order" or maximum chaos.

This sense of directionality of time can be observed in the game of billiards. If we see pool balls scatter from a neat triangle into random areas of the table, we have a sense that time is flowing in a natural way. Should we observe all fifteen balls move around the table and come together to form a neat little triangle, we would feel as if we were watching a movie run backwards. A deck of cards does not easily jump back into the box from which it came.

In the world around us, however, we also see trends towards "order." Crystals, which are very ordered lattices of atoms and molecules, grow spontaneously. And everywhere we observe the ordered dynamics of life forms such as plants and animals.

These brief reflections make one wonder about the existence of an "arrow of time" in our lives. Are we making some kind of progress, do we have a forward direction?

Perhaps it is helpful to view our situation as follows: the more we add to or enforce our habits of ignoring our nature "as it is," the more we travel backwards; the more we familiarize ourselves with and honor our true nature, the more we "move forwards" in time, the more we make progress.

And once we come to know who we are, as the dance of time itself, the concept of direction begins to appear meaningless. The essence of time has nothing to do with direction. One may even argue that direction only arises through the play of time. From the perspective of experience, "dimensionality" is a product of considerations carried through time.

The more we discover and attend to the time aspect of our experience, the more we come to know the self-liberation of all which arises through time. This in turn leads to a relaxation of the rigid concepts and restrictive postures which we have assumed with respect to our own dynamic nature. In the very midst of the concepts of who and what we are, right in the thoughts themselves, we can touch the essence of time.

And in touching the essence of time, we begin to touch the essence of our lives, the essence of mind.

> *Coming and going, life and death:*
> *A thousand hamlets, a million houses.*
> *Don't you get the point?*
> *Moon in the water, blossom in the sky.*
>
> *Gizan*

Responsibility

*We can begin to do something of meaning
By attending to our lives and
Cultivating an understanding of
Who and what we are.*

The Law of Cause and Effect

Realizing the invaluable opportunity of our present life and the hopelessness of pursuing worldly accomplishments, we must decide what to do. Now that we have come to live, what are we to do?

We can begin to do something of meaning by attending to our lives and cultivating an understanding of who and what we are. With sensitivity and kindness, we can begin to directly investigate the nature of our mind and experience. No one else can do this for us; we alone must make this effort. And in making this effort we have tapped into the wisdom of life itself.

In our lives there is a practical principle that is readily evident in our environment. It is one that we recognize at a very young age and is usually referred to as the "law of cause and effect." Actions and events in the world have causes and effects. Eventually we come to recognize that this law applies not only to physical events but also to more personal ones. Our understandings, our aspirations, our wishes, our efforts, our idleness, our thoughts, as well as our personal actions, all have effects.

If we act in a manner which is based on ignoring who we are, then we immediately reinforce the dynamics associated with the emergence of that ignoring. For example, by injuring someone deliberately, emotionally or physically, besides causing suffering to them, we also reinforce and strengthen our habit of ignoring the value of life. The wagon wheels of our journey in life sink deeper into the ground and the wheels are further inclined to go in the direction of the grooves which are formed. This is an immediate effect and most significant for us. In addition, of course, the person we injure may in turn injure us or our loved ones.

By strengthening the emergence of ignorance in our life, we suffer the consequences of that ignorance, both immediately and in the future. If we live in this fashion, the effects of ignorance will manifest endlessly. However, if we practice remembering who we are, we will benefit from that remembrance, both immediately and in the future.

We should begin to recognize the remarkable power which every one of our aspirations, efforts, and actions carries with it, possessing either the power to take us further from ourselves or to return us to who we are. We may define virtuous activity as that which acts to return us to who we are and to eliminate the cycle of suffering and non-virtuous activity as that which tends to reinforce the cycle of ignoring and suffering.

Six Perfections of Virtuous Living

According to the mind teachings, the following six perfections of virtue are regarded as essential for progressing toward wholesome living and honoring who we are: generosity, ethical behavior, effort, patience, meditation, and wisdom.

In the practice of generosity we engender the causes of happiness and remove the causes of suffering. It seems that generosity often expresses itself best simply from living and acting with mindfulness, caring, and kindness in whatever situation we encounter.

Ethical behavior includes such things as practicing non-injury, truthfulness, non-stealing, non-coveting, non-clinging to sensory objects or events, etc. Ultimately all ethical behavior is based on recognizing and respecting the value of all life.

Effort means taking responsibility for one's life and working at developing an understanding of it, ultimately living in accord with what one discovers. Patience refers to the fact that one does this forever since there is no end to the cycle of suffering and the return to ignorance unless one sees to it that there is an end.

Meditation is learning how to rest the mind in its own nature, developing an understanding of that nature, and becoming completely familiar with that nature, whether sitting, sleeping, eating or walking.

Wisdom means realizing the self-liberated quality of everything in our lives, both the waves and ocean of mind, and sharing this realization with everyone by living it.

These are only brief summaries of the six perfections of the practice of virtue in life. Success in these for most of us begins in one place only. Effort.

Making an endless effort at ethical behavior and meditation we discover wisdom, the union of awareness of things "as they are" and loving kindness.

Making an effort now and always, regardless of how much, whether "small" or "large," is essential. Virtue cannot be measured. Every act of virtue is vast. Placing a cup on the shelf with caring and awareness can be as much a practice of virtue as presenting "awakened teachings" to millions of people. In even these busy times, we may bring forth the highest virtue if we lead our lives with kindness and awareness.

But, practically speaking, what is the essence of the practice of virtue? The answer to this is mindfulness, attending to what one is doing, where one is. All of the above six perfections stem from the well-spring of mindfulness. How is mindfulness achieved? By consistent, gentle effort, until it acquires the ease of familiarity. Like learning how to read, eventually it becomes effortless to us.

Once achieved, how is it maintained? Through caring and kindness. By never forgetting its importance, mindfulness is preserved. And in being preserved, mindfulness returns us to our intrinsic awareness, our true nature.

This mindfulness is not extra sharp, like focusing rays of light with a set of lenses into a clean, crisp beam. Rather it is like the sun itself, shining forth with ease, spontaneously as it is. This is a mindfulness of ease.

Mindfulness, awareness, and caring are at the core of virtuous living. Easing these consistently into our lives, we come to realize the wisdom-life of mind itself.

Complete Intimacy

Often in our lives we may wonder how we came to our present condition. Why were we born of a poor family or a wealthy one? Why are we and those around us always having health problems or in good health? Why were we born at a time of peace or war? We cannot answer these questions. Even theories which state that "the events of our life are the results of our previous actions" seem meaningless here.

Certainly there is cause and effect. But, for example, to regard a woman who is born with blindness as responsible for her own blindness, may misrepresent the situation entirely and could be like putting salt on a wound. Cause and effect are hard to fathom; we should not jump to conclusions. Rather, it may be more accurate to view cause and effect as linking everything in the universe to everything else.

Whatever our condition, we must let the truth of our lives, the meaning of our lives blossom forth in it. Regardless of the origin of our condition, we remain responsible for seeing through our condition into its essential nature.

Regardless of its color and shape, its stature and qualities, our condition is nothing other than the expression of our mind, as freedom, completely beyond concepts of it. To cling to theories of origin and cessation does disservice to our mind "as it is." This way of understanding only serves to reinforce restrictive views of mind itself.

But still we may feel compelled to ask how we came to this condition? We may debate endlessly whether or not we are responsible for the causes of our condition and still make no genuine progress. Perhaps the most accurate answer to this question is that we sustain our condition now and it sustains us. In the present moment we are fully responsible for it and it is responsible for us. A completely shared responsibility.

I would not exist if it were not for you. You would not exist if it were not for me. There is a Zen poem which expresses the idea "the mountain depends on the cloud." All interrelated, all given together, present, past or future, here or there. Most are familiar with the fact that some mountains are large enough to create "their own weather," and a cloud which enwraps a mountain may depend on that mountain. It is a little different from our conventional view of cause and effect to consider whether it is also true that the mountain depends on the cloud. However, from the perspective of our experience we will find that the mountain's grandeur does depend on the clouds which embrace it and provide an element of stark contrast.

Completely interrelated, we are fully responsible for ourselves and for everyone else. Everyone is responsible for us. Maintaining the wisdom-life of awakened mind, it is maintained for everyone.

If we think we can be happy independent of others, what a deception! Yesterday, I said an unkind word to a friend and felt miserable. My friend's suffering is my own. If we do not recognize this interdependence, we are missing something. If we are beyond this, to where have we gone? Meditating in the retreat hut or in the bedroom, everyone meditates with us. If we feel our happiness does not depend on others, we don't realize how everything depends on everything else. We are complete intimacy. The universe right now!

Whether or not we agree with this concept of interrelatedness or discover this sense of intimacy, we must take complete responsibility for our role in life at this very moment. We cannot deny our responsibility, regardless of our condition.

We may feel that the rich and powerful in our society have a greater responsibility than we do. How can we, immersed in illness and poverty or just barely able to make a living, do anything more? Yet, when it comes to the meaning of life, our burden is equally great, and the opportunity to discover that meaning may be even greater.

When we recognize the importance of our own effort, we may actually be able to make some progress. We can work to change things. Eventually we may even come to recognize how this effort also depends on "effortlessness." Our effort is none other than the universe's effort. We can rest in our nature regardless of whatever condition we may manifest, effort or non-effort. With or without effort, we live another day, another day lives us. This kind of effort may be called a most excellent effort.

Today I am tired and go to bed early. In the morning I am refreshed. This is a most excellent effort. Nothing is lacking in it. And in doing so, all virtue is maintained.

> *On wide waters, alone, my boat*
> *Follows the current, deep/shallow, high/low.*
> *Moved, I raise my flute to the moon,*
> *Piercing the autumn sky.*

> *Honei*

An Ocean of Suffering

Accepting this
  "I don't want to die,"
From the heart,
  Everything is possible.

The Truth of Suffering

There are times when it feels as if the whole world were undergoing calamity after calamity. Masses of people's lives are extinguished in just one typhoon and then major earthquakes occur in region after region. These are then followed by a fierce battle somewhere or the start of a new plague, and there seems to be no end to the disasters.

We do not need to look at natural or man-made catastrophes to appreciate how widespread suffering is. Even in more favorable times great suffering seems to be everywhere. Mental illness, AIDS, cancer, trauma, poverty, bewilderment, mass murders...

The leaves are spread onto madness!

Even in times of peace and prosperity, how many people do we know who live courageously, fully, vividly, sensitively? How many are happy with their work, their family, their health, their weight, their looks, their character, their income? Tormented by pain, hunger, thirst, fear, jealousy, envy, aversion, desire, birth, aging, illness, and death, the faces of human suffering are more numerous than grains of sand on the earth

We are so fragile, like bubbles, or reflections on the water. And since we cling to the bubbles or reflections, we suffer.

What are the bubbles? What are these reflections? The reflections on the water cry out "I am more than just reflections!" and the ocean answers this cry with silence. In some respects, this silence is a most meaningful answer.

If we have discovered the value and responsibility of life, then we have begun to turn towards the meaning of it. Still, according to traditional teachings, the import of this may remain murky unless we also reflect on the pervasiveness of suffering, our own suffering, that of our parents, our friends, our fellow beings. Seeing this, we can't help but be moved toward embracing action. By reflecting in this way, we can actually develop compassion as strong as that of a mother who helps her ill child by sitting up night after night caring for it.

Perhaps we recall that, in our lives, we once became aware of this pervasive suffering and that somehow we have numbed ourselves to it. We have decided to seek numbness, the suffering is too great. Or perhaps we became so frightened by this suffering that we now avoid it or hide behind a false sense of optimism. We may even deny its existence or dismiss considerations of it as the talk of pessimists saying "the glass is half empty." Or we may dwell on it in despair, proclaiming all as hopeless. There are many avenues open to us here.

However, with time, a cataclysm will come to each and every one of us. If we don't acknowledge the pervasiveness of suffering, we are deceiving ourselves, as if closing our eyes or putting our heads in the sand. And with this we fail to fully take up the responsibility of our lives.

Becoming Friends with Anguish

What father doesn't grieve at the illness or death of his child? He who thinks that enlightenment will spare him from this grief has only imaginary enlightenment as his goal. A father and child are one, and when the child is ill, the father grieves.

We should not shun this grief, nor try to suppress or extinguish it. This grief is in our heart and our heart is in our grief.

And even here we should realize essence of mind, without manufacturing it. Essence of mind...grieving mind, no difference.

Here the entire universe is at rest.

There was once a Zen teacher who achieved a realization of the highest order. In his old age, somehow he was taken over by madness. Now we may come to question both the depth and stability of his original realization. At the same time, we should consider whether it is possible that he achieved the supreme realization and still went mad? Why do we impose so many constraints on the meaning of realization?

In this life we experience having a "body." With this body we will feel pain, whether we are liberated or not. And if the "body" goes mad, then our thinking "goes mad." However, as we become increasingly familiar and accustomed to recognizing "mind as it is," we may be able to maintain our freedom even as our body or our ability to reason fails.

Enlightened living is timeless and beyond our characterizations of it. Even when fully stabilized, it may not be discernible to an outside observer and thus may also appear to come and go. It can be both beyond time and space and fully present within the condition of our existence.

The story of the old Zen master, who upon the approach of his death shouted out "I don't want to die!" always had personal significance to me. His students were quite distressed about this statement at the time. This was no way for a Zen teacher to behave! They asked him to pull himself together for the sake of his students and whether he would offer any other final death poem more becoming of a Zen master to honor them. His only response in return was "Really, I don't want to die."

This is a fully enlightened statement, suffering yet beyond suffering. It should serve as an example for us all. Very simple, very direct. Accepting this "I don't want to die," right from the heart, everything is possible.

And the universe is in awe.

Samsara, nirvana, ignorance, enlightenment, heaven, and hell. Do not fabricate a distinction for a moment!

Although everything is terrible, we live and practice a little bit of virtue. Although everything is perfect as it is, we live and practice a little bit of virtue.

And when our practice is complete, it will not even have a hint of practice or virtue left in it.

It accommodates our life completely. All aspects of it. Even our patterns of delusion can be self-liberated. Our daily life can become our practice totally. This may happen very simply and directly. It does not require religious props. Of course, religious props can benefit us. But they can also mislead us so if we use them to support our efforts, we must use them with the greatest care.

Freedom from suffering does not involve some imagined self going to an imagined land, say Heaven or Dewachen. It involves discovering that freedom right now in the midst of the suffering itself. Even as we cry or long for joy for ourselves and others, right there is our freedom.

In our life, this suffering, everyone's suffering, can work to overcome our laziness and get us out of bed. When our child has a high fever and calls for us for the tenth time in the middle of the night, we get up and go to her, or we bring her into our bed.

This wake up call can inspire us to cut the ties to the cycle of ignoring and return us to seeing fully, to living fully, to suffering fully. When we suffer fully, right there is our freedom!

Having tasted suffering, we move from "mind turns to truth" to "truth becomes our path." The cycle of ignoring has lost its firm grip upon us and we truly begin to lead wholesome and complete lives.

> *The great poisoned drum*
> *Quakes earth, heaven.*
> *Turn back, look—*
> *Dead bodies miles around.*
>
> *Myotan*

Truth Becomes Our Path

Awakened Mind, Awakened Living

Taking care of the yard,
    Sharing a few extra tomatoes
We can express our commitment
To awakened mind.

What Can I Do?

By having begun to appreciate the extreme value of our life, the depth of suffering and ignorance it is subject to, and our responsibility in the emergence of this ignorance and suffering, we feel the urgent need to do something about it. We may ask "What can I do?"

According to the mind teachings, we can begin by attending to and cultivating a commitment to "awakened mind," "awakened living." This commitment can be expressed not only in our practice of virtue but also in directly making efforts to get to know who we are. At this point we may recognize our mind to be the basis of the universe of our experience, the ground of our suffering and liberation, the root of our ignorance and awareness. Thus we have begun to realize the importance of coming to know and understand mind

In our life we have come to mistake the various projections or conceptual abstractions of mind for ourselves, identifying with the waves of mind without regard to its depths. Living subject to these deceptions, we find ourselves tormented by conflicting emotions, subject to birth, aging, illness, and death.

It is said we are like children of wealthy parents who roam about the slums unaware of our inherited riches. Though we swim in fresh water, we suffer from thirst, never daring to take a drink.

Having achieved the greatest treasure of all time, a human birth, we still strive for recognition and honor by our fellow people. Though we are fully endowed with the wealth of human faculties, we covet other people's things, positions, and experience.

In spite of all this, somehow we may be fortunate enough to realize the importance of knowing who we are. We must come to know who we are! This is the beginning of commitment to awakened mind. And mind itself serves as the base, the way, and the fruit of this commitment.

With Complete Confidence, a Commitment to Waking Up

Our commitment to awakened mind, awakened living, may cause us to investigate and follow what may be call "awakened teachings" or "awakened teachers or companions." Awakened teachings can come from limitless places and in limitless forms but they are only awakened when they speak truth to us, when they speak our truth. This truth is never sectarian or doctrinal. It must ask us to look at our situation with open minds and open hearts. And based on this looking, we may eventually come to discover true faith or confidence.

This faith is never a blind one according to awakened teachings. It develops from our thorough investigations and reflections, although it is by no means limited to the results of these inquiries. Ultimately confidence or faith may be said to come from awakened mind itself; confidence is the expression of our awakened mind. Having discovered a deep faith, we are saturated through and through.

The crisis of our life is extreme in nature. It is as if we were born at a time when there is a great cause and, like Moses, we were asked to lead everyone from bondage into freedom. Slavery is still rampant, although we may remain unaware of it. We and countless other beings are slaves to our own misunderstandings, our delusions, and the conflicting emotions which arise from them. How can we remain complacent?

This is the call of awakened mind. Come to know who you are and in knowing this be free. Every moment of our lives we can take up this fight against slavery, this call to truth. With this attitude, truth can become our path, completely.

We cling to our suffering since it stems from the core of that which we hold on to so dearly, our self-image. Somehow we elect not to be free, not to be responsible. It is so much easier to assume we are not responsible for our own state and for the state of our companions. After all, we were not chosen to be spiritual leaders, nor were we given the opportunity to become doctors. We prefer to call this someone else's responsibility.

But this responsibility begins and ends with us. It also begins and ends in the little things. In how we live from moment to moment.

There is nothing big that we have to do. Although we may wish to bring everyone to an awakened state by preaching wonderful sermons or exhibiting magical powers, we will be unable to do so.

Indeed, we may come to realize that only in living with virtue in our lives, directly and immediately, can the entire universe be liberated. This liberation is not just a fiction or wishful thinking, but can be a very real part of our lives and our experience. Taking care of the yard, sharing the extra tomatoes with the neighbors, we can express our commitment to awakened mind. Extending a word of genuine kindness here and there, everything is saved.

Our responsibility is simply to live this truth in our daily condition, this commitment to knowing and honoring that which we are.

Once we begin to realize the depths of our being, we can also begin to trust all of our life, even the reflections on its waves. We can be ordinary again, without a sense of contrived spirituality. In this manner, we deal with the great crisis directly and appropriately. No longer trying to grab the tiger by the tail, we can work with the tiger most effectively and with full presence of mind. And in this way, we can make some genuine progress in our understanding and in bringing that understanding to bear in our lives.

Eating breakfast — "here," a job we hate from 8:00 a.m. to 7:00 p.m. — "in between," and a baseball game — "over there;" this may be the substance of our lives. This substance can be mired in our delusions or it can be fully included in our enlightenment. Right here is the great crisis. What do we do with it?

All this can be idleness or it can be the expression of awakened mind. It depends on us.

Nothing inside,
Light is my pocket.
The evening's cool!

Old Japanese Haiku Poem

The Importance of Happiness

It is the thirst for happiness
That can guide us
To live wholeheartedly in the present life,
As the one we are right now.

The Great Wish

All beings wish to be happy; so what else is new? This has been such a common proclamation over the history of mankind that it is easy to dismiss it as trivial. In fact, as human beings this thirst for happiness is an extremely important issue. It is this thirst which causes us to do things in our life. It is this thirst which causes us to look for who we are. It is this thirst which teaches us to care for life. Ultimately, it is this thirst that can guide us to live wholeheartedly in the present life, as the one we are right now.

Our happiness can become a complete guide to wholesome living, to living our life courageously, unabashed. Similarly, our dissatisfaction can help to remind us that there is something in our lives which needs to be addressed.

Today, in North America we have a unique opportunity to realize the import of happiness. By recognizing the basic rights of most of its citizens, based on the principles of equality and freedom, this democratic and free society has embarked on the road to happiness. Still, however, we are beset by many social injustices and other difficulties. Until we realize the meaning of happiness on a personal level, even the institutions of happiness will continue to fail.

By ignoring our dissatisfaction and happiness, we remain caught up in the endless cycles of suffering which we seem to have inherited from somewhere.

The path to happiness can begin by attending to our own sense of well-being or dissatisfaction, moment by moment. Attending to our happiness in this way, we may also discover that our happiness and that of others are not independent. Cultivating our happiness goes hand-in-hand with cultivating the joy of those around us.

The Four Immeasurables

In the mind teachings the "four immeasurables" are presented. These are love, compassion, joy, and equanimity.

Love is defined as the wish for all beings to be happy and to have the causes of happiness in their lives. Compassion is the wish for all to be free from their suffering and the causes of suffering in their lives. We take joy at the happiness of others and with equanimity wish for all beings to be happy equally.

We can cultivate the four immeasurables by reflecting on the meaning of each one of them immediately in our lives. Traditionally one begins with developing the last immeasurable first since if we elect to work on love for someone in preference to others we are mixing both virtuous and non-virtuous elements into our practice and it is not as beneficial as it could be.

We begin by reflecting on 1) our strong attachment to self, family, and friends, 2) our indifference and neutrality with regards to certain individuals and groups, and 3) our strong aversion or hatred to other individuals and groups. We tend to have strong attachment to those who are closest to us and value and support us; we tend to have strong aversion to those who threaten us or our family or think poorly of us; we are indifferent to those who do neither. We should reflect on 1) the causes of our attachments, aversions, and neutrality, 2) their stability or instability, and 3) their relationship to self-interest.

Understanding our own bewilderment and our own tendency to perform negative actions in "the wrong situation," we can appreciate the bewilderment of others and understand their negative actions.

Understanding our own wish for happiness, for self-actualization, for comfort and ease, we can come to understand and remember the similar wishes of others. Even as a child we expressed the wish for all to be happy and free from suffering. How is it that we have forgotten this?

As a child we also gave unabashed expression to our self-interests. Early childhood is notorious for being the years of "me" and "mine." And yet at some point we begin to express an interest in others as well as ourselves. On some occasion we may experiment with putting someone else's needs before our own. We can be really moved by the wonder of this. But we are so accustomed to self-cherishing attitudes that we continue to find it difficult to balance our own needs and desires with those of others around us.

Eventually, we come to consider the fact that there are billions of other human beings and many billions of other beings, even in the present time, and that there is only one "me." From this perspective, our self seems almost insignificant and it appears that we have been misplacing our energies. The importance of serving others is awakened. But again we are so accustomed with serving our own needs that it requires a very real effort to overcome the easy self-serving ways of our childhood.

How do we work to have some positive impact on all others throughout time and space? We can begin to do this now by cherishing each and every person or animal we encounter. The importance of this practice cannot be overemphasized. Simple to explain, it takes effort to put into practice. This valuing of others, balanced with a valuing of self, can be a very real practice for us. And when coupled with the hardships of following this path, our life takes on a rich meaning.

According to Tibetan tradition, we should apply the wish for happiness and freedom from suffering in our daily life, in all our bodily actions, in all our speech, and in all our thoughts, whatever our condition and circumstances may be. We make our best effort, whether small or large. The measure of our effort is not at all the issue and is beyond comparison. Our effort may entail just holding enough of a job to provide for ourselves and our family; or just enough effort to take care of ourselves within the context of consideration for others.

Among Tibetans it is taught that even the act of breathing should be utilized to develop this altruistic attitude.

We can begin a meditation practice on this by imagining all beings throughout space and time as being here with us, in our present space. Understanding our own bewilderment, we genuinely feel the suffering of all these beings which can take a vast multitude of forms. With each inhalation we take in the suffering as visualized black smoke directly into the center of our heart (at the "heart center" right in front of our spine, at the middle of our chest). As we breathe out, we joyfully wish to give all beings a deep happiness, and in so doing, the blackness in our heart, including our self-cherishing attitude and grasping, are transformed into brilliant rays of pure light. These rays then go out to all beings transforming their suffering into great satisfaction and wholesome being.

First we meditate on the suffering of all others and from the naturally arising compassion we gladly take on their suffering; then we meditate on our own great inner happiness, independent of our condition, and from the naturally arising love we offer our happiness to all freely.

It is interesting to note that, contrary to common belief, the Tibetan teachers do not regard this meditation as benefitting other sentient beings directly in the moment. They are very explicit about this being a mental practice and that, as such, it will not benefit others directly. However, this practice does develop our attitude and motivation, and stabilize our minds with respect to the engendered attitude.

By developing such extraordinary positive tendencies, they will manifest later in our lives in very direct and tangible ways. Thus in this practice we are accumulating the causes of virtue. In addition to planting the seeds which will sprout in the future, through this practice we actual start to honor, in the present, our true nature in the continuum of our being. And by doing this practice, we train our mind to rest in the midst of the activities of the meditation.

By doing this practice for the benefit of all, not just for one or select individuals, we develop our motivation and accumulate the seeds of virtue in a very effective way.

This practice of "taking in suffering and giving out happiness" works in simple and direct ways which can be observed from our immediate experience. When truly joyous ourselves, it radiates to everyone in the room. When we come in contact with someone else's suffering, we suffer ourselves. When we trust in our own nature, this confidence comforts others.

With this care our happiness can become quite vast, immeasurable, embracing our life totally. We can begin to look for satisfaction in our lives in a comprehensive manner. Instead of tying our happiness to our condition, our honor, our recognition, our wealth, our health, we can touch a deeper joy. A happiness which embraces all of the human condition. A happiness which is deeply rooted, relaxed, naturally present; not fabricated and frivolous.

Our wish for happiness can act as a rudder for our life. Our efforts to achieve happiness, for ourselves and for others, can become a way of life. Remembering this as our path, we become like eagles soaring in the sun. We have begun to live completely.

And in doing so, we have settled into the vastness of life itself.

> *A water bird comes and goes,*
> *Leaving no traces at all.*
> *Yet it knows*
> *How to go its own way.*
>
> Zen Poem

Dispelling Confusion From Our Path

Touching Restful Mind

Sitting, standing, walking, living,
Open and relaxed, fresh,
With nothing to attain and
    Nothing to avoid,
Loose and natural,
Let awareness settle into its own nature;
    No going astray.

Let It Be

Meditation practice is very simple and encompasses all of our life. Through the practice of meditation, we begin to develop an understanding of the nature of mind. Eventually, we can get in touch with the "essence" of mind and learn to live in accord with it. Finally, we can come to know essence of mind intimately and thoroughly, throughout all of life's conditions and displays.

To develop a sense of our natural awareness, it is usually helpful to begin with sitting practice. Begin by assuming a posture which is firm and pleasant.

Traditionally, emphasis is placed on allowing the backbone to be comfortably straight. In addition, if you are on the ground, cross your legs or if you are on a chair, place your feet flat on the floor. Then rest your hands on your knees, palm downwards, or rest them in your lap, palm upwards. Gaze softly at the space of the floor, at about a distance of three feet in front of you. Eyelids are kept about half open and importance is placed on the instruction that the eyes should not wander.

The meditation posture should neither promote restlessness nor sleepiness.

Next sit without thinking about the past or the future. This includes not thinking about what you have done yesterday or twenty years ago and not thinking about what you are going to do tomorrow or what state you will achieve during the meditation. Do not evaluate even your present experience. Just let awareness settle into its own nature, free from fabrication.

This is a gentle practice. As various thoughts of the past, present, or future arise, do not dwell on them nor suppress them. Just let them be.

If you become slightly sleepy or dull, make a slightly greater effort. If you become slightly restless, or the mind is somewhat wild, just relax a bit.

On the other hand, if you are very sleepy, it might be good to try one or more of the following: 1) open the eyes slightly more, 2) attend to the light and space qualities of experience, 3) if warm, open a window slightly, 4) get up and stretch a little. If possible, try looking out over a vista or even sprinkle cold water on your face. If these don't do the trick, go take a nap. Similarly, if you are too restless and strongly being carried away by thoughts, it might be good to close the eyes a little more, attend to the darker and denser qualities of experience, put on a sweater, go do some exercise, or take a strenuous walk.

If you become caught up in or lost in your dullness or restlessness, apply a remedy. Otherwise just sit relaxed and open.

According to the mind teachings there are three stages to meditation practice. At first mind is like a stream rushing down a mountain gorge. Later mind is more like a wide river flowing on a plain, perhaps like the Mississippi. And finally, it is like an unusually calm ocean, accompanied by a sense of familiarity, as when a daughter reunites with her mother.

Before we begin a meditation session, in the beginning, it is helpful to select a quiet and peaceful place with a minimum of distractions. Then we start the sitting by reflecting for a moment on the virtue of our life or the virtue of practicing meditation.

What are the virtues of meditation?

It is taught that of the six perfections, meditation is the most important and sitting practice is most helpful at developing meditation in our lives. Traditionally, endless benefits due to meditation are espoused including, eventually, complete freedom from suffering.

It is important to investigate whether or not meditation has any value early on in our practice. If we observe a value, observe that it adds significance to our lives and allows us to see things more clearly, then we should acknowledge this. Seeing our situation more clearly, we also see the situations of others more clearly and are better able to be with them or help them.

We each have different reasons for sitting. We may find that when we don't sit, we tend to get more caught up in our personal craziness. Or we may just feel as if our life has no meaning. In sitting, our life becomes meaningful; we begin to step into the meaning of life itself.

After thinking about the virtue of meditation, just let our awareness be as it is and let go of all thoughts about the past, present or future. Here it is important not to try too hard. Also, having thought about the benefit of meditation, here it is important to drop our expectations, not to expect too much.

❀

Some Additional Practices

If you are unable to settle the mind through the above practice, try other practices. Select a visual object on which to place your attention, such as a pebble or cobble. It is particularly helpful in the beginning to investigate whether or not we can settle the mind on an "object." If we can't settle our mind on an object, it will be difficult to settle our awareness into itself. Here, just simply attend to the object of choice, without analyzing it or thinking about it. When distracted from the object, gently return to it. According to these teachings, when mind rests on an object, without distraction, then we are doing what is called "resting our mind in its own nature."

If this doesn't work, try settling mind by working with attending to breath. Here, just breathe naturally through the nose and attend to the rich sensations and experience of breathing, including the exhalation, pause, inhalation and pause. This practice is very effective if you find yourself overly distracted by your thoughts.

Why do we begin meditation practice with settling our mind or resting mind? Only when the mind is calm, can one begin to see clearly. At that time we no longer see subject to the flickering lamp of our thoughts but can begin to experience in a first hand and direct way. Thus we can provide a firm basis for further investigations into the nature of our mind. So in this approach to meditation, it is usual to begin with settling the mind, with touching the restful aspect of mind.

When Does Mind Rest?

What is this restful or tranquil mind? It is not like the rest of sleep, but more like the calm of the archer just before releasing the arrow. It has been described as the state of nakedness which arises when startled by a loud sound, for example, by two wooden blocks coming together. When we discover this tranquility, whether in sitting or in our daily lives, we are able to see and hear more vividly, peacefully, clearly. We are more relaxed and open with our environment and our friends. We develop a sense of ease in our lives.

Six Powers and the Essence of Practice

Traditionally there are six powers which lead to successful practice. They are referred to as the powers of 1) hearing (the instructions on the meditation), 2) reflecting (on these instructions), 3) mindfulness, 4) vigilant awareness (or detecting distraction or dullness), 5) joyous effort and 6) complete familiarity.

Just as a fire will not start by rubbing two sticks together with frequent interruptions so, it is said, we will not come to discover the serene mind unless we apply ourselves consistently.

The essence of practice is further described as having three aspects, whether sitting or engaged in daily life's activities. The first and most important is mindfulness, which is described as not forgetting the object of concentration. When not sitting, we may maintain this by just putting our attention on whatever we are doing.

The second element of practice is vigilant awareness, which involves knowing what is going on at all times, recognizing when we are caught up in distraction or dullness. When not sitting, we practice this by recognizing when we lose awareness of what is going on and returning to what we are doing with presence of mind, whether eating, walking, cleaning toilets, or doing anything.

The third element of practice is caring, taking care of how we act and what we do. Here we attend to every situation, every person, every emotion we encounter with care. Just as in the earlier discussion on the four immeasurables emphasis was placed on valuing each being we encounter, here we extend this attitude to all which transpires in our life.

With proper mindfulness, that is natural mindfulness, not contrived but shining like the rays of the sun, vigilant awareness and caring will naturally arise. And through these all of the six perfections enter our lives in a deep way.

Cutting Up the Pie into Nine Stages

According to all the meditation schools of Tibet, there are nine stages to discovering the tranquility of mind. They may be described briefly as 1) "settling or placing mind," in which we realize the wildness of mind, 2) "continually settling or placing mind," where one discovers the possibility for serenity, 3) "immediately resettling mind," where one develops skill at recognizing the emergence of distractions and dullness, 4) "closely settling or placing mind," where one discovers the ability to settle the mind intensely, 5) "taming mind," where one discovers the importance of practicing virtue and meditation, 6) "peaceful mind," where one is clear about the negative qualities of obscurations, 7) "completely peaceful mind," where one no longer thirsts for or avoids what is or what is not, 8) "one pointedness," where we almost effortlessly settle mind, and 9) "placing mind equally," where everything in our life is illuminated effortlessly and naturally.

These nine stages can be useful guideposts for our practice, as can be the corresponding powers. It is said that the power of hearing takes us through the first stage, the power of reflecting helps us through the second stage, the power of mindfulness through the fourth stage, the power of vigilant awareness through the sixth stage, the power of effort through the eighth stage, and the power of complete familiarity through the ninth stage. Also our attentiveness is described to be "disciplined" in the first two stages, "interrupted" from the third to seventh stage, "uninterrupted" in stage eight and effortless or "naturally present" in stage nine.

Regardless of which description we find most suitable for our experience, the primary effort is to develop a balance between being too tight about our practice and being too loose. At the same time, we should not be discouraged if our mind is too wild or elated if it rests easily. We only need to have some sense of the serene aspect of our mind and some stability to pursue our investigations of mind in an effective manner.

As we integrate resting mind practice with the dawning of insight, we will begin to regard all thoughts and distractions as important elements of our meditation practice, and not things to be avoided. Nothing has to happen in our practice; everything is perfect just as it is. So here we should let go of our hopes and fears and just attend to the practice itself. These stages are not meant to be a ladder to climb, but rather a guidepost for successful practice, should we wonder how to make our own practice succeed.

If you have elected to work with an object or breath, that is perfectly fine, but at some point it is important to return to meditation without the assistance of an object or a reference frame. Eventually, it is important to learn to settle awareness into its own space without reliance upon an object.

This space is intensely alive and completely free from dullness. The greatest obstacles to succeeding in practice are described to be laziness or unwillingness to practice, forgetting or altering the instructions, wildness and dullness, non-application of remedies when appropriate, and over-application of remedies. We must learn to work with all of these.

With sustained practice, eventually we may experience some sensations or experiences of bliss, clarity and non-conceptuality. We should not get stuck in any of these states or make them our objective. If these experiences should arise, the essential point is not to attach to them or place undue emphasis on them.

So Now What?

Now that we have this elaborate conceptual framework, how do we proceed with meditation?

After we have learned to strike a balance between exertion and relaxation, we no longer have to strive at increasing our mindfulness. Unless one loses one's attentiveness or alertness, and thus begins to wander in conceptual journeys and existence, there is nothing to do but relax.

If we try to tie down a camel, it is a stubborn thing which attempts to go every-which-way; but once we drop the cord, it stands still, where it is.

So just sit, just live, with mind relaxed and open, and apply mindfulness and vigilant awareness as necessary. Even as thoughts arise and grasping arise, we may discover that the flavor of tranquility is not lost. Meditation can then embrace all of our life completely, our feelings, our passions, our fears, our anger, our thoughts, our identity; nothing is left out.

If our meditation is just another tool used to add to or remove things from the experiences of our life, or even worse, a basis for arrogance and feelings of superiority, it can do us more harm than good. When it becomes simply an expression of who we are, moment by moment, it can become the true way by which we discover and maintain the wisdom-life of our mind.

His eye is a shooting star,
His spirit is lightning.
A sword to kill,
A sword to give life.

Mumon

Discovering Mind

Looking at mind directly, again and again,
*   We come to know,*
With certainty,
*   That it is unborn and without substance.*
Nothing can be added or taken away.

All thoughts and appearances,
*   Just the dynamic play of mind.*
Waves of the ocean, all of one flavor.
*   Indestructible, open space.*
Knowing one thing,
*   We come to know all things.*

What is there left to fear?
*   No going astray.*

Looking at Calm Mind with Fresh Vision

Having learned to place the mind on an object and settle it into its own awareness, we have created a basis for investigating the mind directly. Like preparing a laboratory for a controlled experiment in which only one variable or set of variables is investigated at a time, we have eliminated the winds of conceptual bias. We have learned to see vividly and with fresh vision once again, and seeing clearly we can look directly at whom and what we are.

So after we have discovered our calm mind, beyond the whirlpools of thought, and have become somewhat stable in it, we begin by placing our mind in this state. We sit as before, with an awareness as calm and clear as if we were walking along a plank bridge which spans a small creek. Our posture is the same as before; however, now our eyes are fully open and look straight ahead.

Now consider the following aspects of serene mind.

• Does the resting mind have structure, shape or form? Is it round, or a square, or spherical in form? Does it have length, width, or depth?

• Does the mind have any color? Is it blue, white, green, black, or red? Or is it like a crystal or mirror?

• Does the mind reside in any particular location? If so, where is it found?

• Does the mind exist in any particular time? In which time is it found, does it exist in the past, present, or future? Is there any instant when mind came into being in the past or comes into existence in the present?

• Does the mind have anything serving as a basis for it? Anything physical? Is there any direct evidence of a supporting basis or is this something which only arises through inferences of mind?

• Is the mind an empty void or a luminous void like the sky?

These investigations should be conducted at a leisurely pace until you are certain of your conclusions, until no doubts remain. Any conclusions should be carefully checked.

Conducting these investigations one may discover that certain questions are quite inappropriate, like asking what song does a rainbow sing. Mind certainly does not have a shape or color which can be ascribed to it. It does not have a location in space or a position in time. If we feel that mind is located in our head, then where in the head is it located? How do we explain that the mind knows sensations in our fingers or elsewhere in the body? Why did both the ancient Greeks and the Tibetans conclude that mind is located in the heart?

From an experiential perspective, no location can be determined. No basis for mind can be seen or known directly. However, from an experiential perspective the eye cannot see itself, yet there is a physical basis for the operation of an eye. Similarly, perhaps the mind cannot see itself, yet there may be a physical basis for it.

The intent here is not to get caught up in reasoning about the observations from this investigation although initially this may be helpful to work with our concepts and doubts. This practice is regarded to be most effective by practicing a direct looking, with the mind, toward the answers of the questions posed.

Listening to the cry within us "Who am I?" we look again and again, directly and clearly. Seeing nothing concrete we begin to develop some certainty about the fact that we really are open, timeless, self-luminous, both in our "essence" and within the "periphery" of who we are. These qualities pervade everything; there are no corners left untouched.

We may find that as we practice, we become more aware of a naturally present awareness and luminosity, whenever "we practice mindfulness" or "mindfulness practices us." This awareness itself may become the object of attention until there is certainty as to even its nature.

Once we become certain about what we see, we rest in that certainty. In some ways, during the initial phases of these meditations we are like a bird flapping its wings to reach a height from which it obtains a vast view. Once we achieve the view, we can begin to glide with little or no effort.

Looking at Thoughts and Appearances with Fresh Vision

Now we may also attend to our thoughts (including intense emotions) and then, in turn, to any other appearances before the mind. Is there a form, color, basis, or mode of existence of thoughts or appearances? Do they have a specific location in space where they dwell?

Once again we discover nothing. Are even the appearances of mind devoid of substantive entities? All possess the characteristics of openness, time, luminosity with them, in them.

An important follow-up to these considerations is to meditate on whether or not thoughts, appearances, and our serene mind arise, abide, and cease to exist somehow. These considerations form the basis of an independent meditation practice, one which is regarded to be extremely profound. Even appearances which we have taken to be solid things are found to be open and to not dwell anywhere. Experientially, they are not found to arise from anywhere specifically.

Investigating Moving and Calm Mind

After we have carefully evaluated these matters, we should investigate whether thinking mind or the appearances of mind are the same or different from the serene mind. If they are the same, then why are they discernible as different topics for investigation? If they are different, why do both have no source, dwelling, or destination? Why are both open and self-luminous?

Eventually we may develop some confidence in the discovery that mind's manifestations and essence are one and the same. We may note an inseparable unity to our experience of clarity and emptiness. With this, we begin to relax our incessant and desperate addiction to certain states of mind over other states since all have this same flavor. Also with this, there truly begins to be nothing left to fear; there is nothing which mind can gain or lose. Everything is just the dynamic play of an open awareness empty of any essence. And experience of this play of mind is completely self-liberating and self-illuminating for us.

The analogy presented here is that the mind is like the ocean and the thoughts and appearances are like the waves of the ocean. This at first sounds as if it implies the existence of a substantive medium. However, the existence of such a medium is not supported by our experience. Thus it would be wrong to conclude that there is any substance which underlies mind. Indeed this "open" mind is seen as the basis for all, directly and intimately.

The waves of mind come and go, but the depths remain unscathed, unperturbed, like the sky. Here we can begin to realize the "sky of awareness," indestructible but all accommodating. When we realize that the waves themselves are free of arising, existing and cessation, since nothing ever comes into existence, then even the waves take on the quality of self-liberation, simultaneously with our experience of them.

The Natural Freedom of Mind

We thus begin to realize the natural freedom of our mind, encompassing everything. Having one speck of time, we have all of time. Having one speck of awareness, we have all of awareness. We are the life of the universe and it is the life of us.

To realize this we must go beyond thinking about it and actually step into the stream. Little by little we let go of our incessant identification with the reflections of mind. Our identity now extends beyond those reflections right into the core of life itself.

And in coming to know this, we are liberated right in our daily life, whatever our condition or character. We begin to realize the self-perfection of everything. Our appreciation becomes vast and complete, leaving nothing out. We no longer cling to meditative states of quietness or discriminate harshly between virtue and non-virtue. This self-perfection is virtue itself. Virtuous activity becomes the only possibility for us.

We can preserve this realization by continuing our practice of mindfulness, vigilant awareness, and caring, in an even more continuous and relaxed way. And we can begin to truly live our life, as the one we are right now.

For years I have suffered in snow and frost;
Now I am startled at pussy willows falling.

Zen Comment

Understanding Mind

We come to realize coemergence of
Awareness and openness,
Appearance and openness,
Thoughts and openness.

Relaxing with presence of awareness
Once again we live
In complete intimacy with
The universe.

Coemergence of Awareness and Openness, Appearance and Openness

As we begin to discover the coemergence of awareness and openness, appearances and openness, and thoughts and openness, we also begin to discover the self-liberation and self-perfection of everything which arises. If we fail to understand this about mind and its expressions, we continue to suffer and wander about in all kinds of conceptual existence. When we are aware of mind's emptiness, clarity, and dynamic presenting, we begin to discover the intrinsic freedom of mind.

We may also discover that our knowing and not-knowing arise simultaneously, completely given together. We know and are ignorant at the same time.

This being the situation, how do we develop a decisive understanding of mind "as it is"?

When we look at serene mind directly, and see nothing, still a knowing is present. This knowing is referred to as the coemergence of mind and emptiness, or awareness and openness.

When we look at a thought such as one of severe anger, we do not see a source or dwelling place or destination for the anger. From this we develop a degree of freedom from our anger, it loses some power over us. Having a degree of freedom, we actually have the possibility of complete freedom. This is the coemergence of thoughts and emptiness.

When we look at external appearances, and keep looking, their solidity dissolves. This is the coemergence of appearances and emptiness.

If we observe coemergence and thereafter think, "Ah, this is the coemergence of thoughts and emptiness," this kind of afterthought is actually of no use to us. But if we understand coemergence as expressed above, directly, we are practicing what is called "joining with coemergence," the stream of life itself.

If we feel that "all is emptiness" and thus lose our caring and compassion for events, for others, for ourselves, we are joining with coemergence incorrectly. If we come to believe that our calm and clear mind is the cultivation of understanding of mind, then we are mistaken. Here it is important to even drop the presupposition of "mind" as an entity. When mind itself has been "dropped" or has "disappeared," then we are beginning to develop a profound understanding.

At this stage, conceptualization of the process is not viewed as being very helpful. It only reinforces old ways of looking at things and living, and keeps us from entering the stream of life directly. It is sometimes said that, at this point, the more accurate our map is, the more likely it is that we will go astray, mistaking the map for reality. However, in this tradition, maps are still regarded as extremely precious with respect to helping us arrive at this point and helping us stabilize our realization of it.

Once again, we can preserve the understanding of mind which arises in our sitting meditation by practicing mindfulness, vigilant awareness, and caring, as defined earlier. They serve to keep us from falling back into generating particular thoughts and emotions which may act like thieves, taking us from this treasure of true understanding.

Finally, we may feel as if we enter the level of complete perfection, where everything is liberated as it is. The completeness of everything shines clear of itself. There is nothing left to free or correct. Nothing to realize. Reality shines forth all by itself, without us having to do anything.

And with this everything is preserved.

> *How much more he who turns within*
> *And confirms directly his own nature,*
> *That his own nature is no-nature—*
> *Such has transcended vain words.*
> *The gate opens, and cause and effect are one;*
> *Straight runs the way — not two, not three.*
> *Taking as form the form of no-form,*
> *Going or returning, he is ever at home.*
> *Taking as thought the thought of no-thought,*
> *Singing and dancing, all is the voice of truth.*
> *Wide is the heaven of boundless Samadhi,*
> *Radiant the full moon of the fourfold wisdom.*
> *What remains to be sought?*
> *Nirvana is clear before him,*
> *This very place the Lotus paradise,*
> *This very body the Buddha.*

> *Hakuin Zenji*

Eliminating Misunderstandings

Regarding
  Emptiness as the dissolution of form,
  Form as a hindrance to openness,
We go astray.

Better it is to remain mindful and kind,
  Not trying to replace our ordinary mind
With anything at all.

Levels of Understanding

It is important to be clear about what is meant by understanding mind. Traditionally, three levels of understanding are presented. The first is basically "conceptual understanding," like upon hearing about Yosemite Valley, we may develop some ideas about it. The second level is referred to as "glimpsing understanding," like seeing a few pictures in a book or in a slide show or having a brief visit. The third is called "thorough understanding," like living at a location and getting to know it well. We have gone there ourselves and have become familiar with it on a firsthand basis.

If we do not differentiate between these types of understanding, we may be quite mistaken about where we are at. For example, in reading this book, if we feel we understand what it says because we are considering it carefully, it is important to know that this understanding is on an intellectual or conceptual level. This can be very meaningful for us, but we really haven't taken a drink from the cup of water; we have only read a dissertation on it.

Now if we encounter a genuine practitioner of an awakened lineage and do some practice ourselves or perhaps experience a special insight as a result of a deep shock in our lives, we are beginning to feel the water's wetness and taste it. Finally, if we apply ourselves to these meditations wholeheartedly, we will be doing nothing other than drinking the water and thus have direct experience of it.

Going Astray with Respect to Openness

The greatest potential for going astray with respect to the understanding of emptiness is by beginning to believe that nothing matters anymore. This is a nihilistic view of emptiness and misses the point entirely. Comforting a crying baby by holding her over our heart, how can we say nothing matters? Feeling the adrenaline take over us as we are cut off on the freeway, how can we say nothing matters? This very life is the great matter, in its entirety. It is a most tragic error when we attempt to deny it or dismiss it.

Next we may feel that looking and seeing the empty nature of mind is not doing enough. So we may go on to think about emptiness and "fabricate it." This also misses the point. Recognizing mind essence is the sword which cuts through the turmoil. Why continue to stir up the pot?

Similarly we may feel that when thoughts or difficulties arise we have to relate to them by labeling them as empty. This is also regarded as incorrect practice. The thought or difficulty is empty from the moment it appears; any subsequent labeling process can cause us to live in a very artificial manner.

Or we may come to feel that we must view everything as empty by remembering that it is empty. Actually the correct way to go about this is to simply remain mindful and aware, resting the nature of mind into itself. Here we are again advised not to fabricate openness.

As we progress with practice, we may feel that we have gained many insights into who and what we are. Also we may have some unusual experience of lightness or bliss or luminosity or fear or other things. It is important to not regard these as highlights of our experience or to place undue emphasis on them. Remain unattached to them. Even people who suffer from mental illness see many unusual things and it is their very attachment to those experiences and their significance which brings them so much trouble.

Do not attach to or try to continue any particular experience regardless of how wonderful it is. The mirror quality of our mind is clear when we remain mindful, and it is mindfulness and caring which can help to save us from these errors. We must care enough to maintain mindfulness or all may be lost.

It is remarkable how many practitioners of religious traditions develop a sense of arrogant pride. They become convinced they possess some higher knowledge. How many religious "leaders" are victims of this same error! The truth of our lives is very simple and the way is very direct and clear. No one owns it, no one has a higher knowledge which we must receive from them. Transmission is a simple and direct process.

Whereas the basic instruction is simple and the truth immediately available to us, it is difficult to develop confidence in teachings and practice without the help of a teacher. It is also difficult to recognize and correct errors in practice without the benefit of a teacher. A teacher instills confidence in the mind teachings and in the practice, but still our success depends only our practice.

And through practice, we come to recognize the kindness and openness of mind as the very essence of our teacher.

In Zen one practices by chanting a sutra called the Heart Sutra on a daily basis. In fact, a Zen student is always chanting the Heart Sutra; he or she lives the

Heart Sutra. It is not something that a Zen student has to think about. In Zen, when doing something, the instruction is "just do," if thinking about a million things at one time, just think about a million things at one time.

There is no error in this.

> *Forms don't hinder emptiness,*
>   *Emptiness is the tissue of form;*
> *Emptiness is not dissolution of form,*
>   *Form is the flesh of emptiness.*
> *Inside the Dharma Gates*
>   *Where form and emptiness are-not-two,*
> *A lame turtle with painted eyebrows*
>   *Stands in the evening breeze.*

> *Hakuin Zenji*

Confusion Arises
as
Pristine Awareness

Bringing Illness and Death to the Path

From the perspective of experience
There arises only aliveness;
Only our thoughts speak of the dead.

Stepping into the nature of mind itself
No birth, no existence, no death.
Just complete intimacy.

Bringing Death to the Path

From the perspective of experience, there is only aliveness. Only our thoughts speak of the dead.

But what about our personal death?

Certainly our body will die and with that so will our capacity to interact with others in the ways we have become accustomed to. Having known individuals who have suffered a deterioration of their mental capacities, we can infer that even our personal mind will die or be so transformed by death that we will not remain the "same person." Look at how different we are now compared to when we were tiny children. Even during our conventional lifetime, we change a lot. We must come to terms with the fact that we, as our personal existence, will change radically. This we know with certainty.

We may hope for heavens to go off into or fear imagined hells, but even if we visit these places in a dream or in a vision, we cannot know whether they exist independent of our brain's capacity to organize the play of space, time and awareness.

So how can we relate to the fact that we will die?

It is important to approach death by not regarding it as something that will happen to an imagined self sometime in an imagined future. Instead, just as any tragedy or event in our lives happens "now" to us, so our dying will take place in the present. So we should begin to understand how to relate to dying by remembering that it will take place in the present and not in some distant future.

Once we become clear on this, we can relate to death in a more effective and immediate way, one which will help to prepare us for "the event."

By understanding mind in the present, we will also understand the mind of dying. By getting to know the endless transformations and dynamics of mind we can come to know dying on a first hand basis, very intimately. Realizing that there is no core to our individual existence other than indestructible mind itself, we can relax a little about all this. Having discovered the non-existence of body and mind, we begin to settle in the indestructible mind itself.

With awareness of the interplay of space and time, we have begun to deeply appreciate our life. This appreciation can extend through our life into all of its events including illness and death.

This is not to imply that when we get ill or realize that we are near death, we will not suffer. It has been said that fear of death can arise even in the wisest of beings. However, accompanying that fear and suffering there will be a degree of freedom from that fear and suffering. Depending on what we have realized, this degree of freedom may actually seem vast, and in comparison, our fear will seem quite insignificant. If we have truly discovered the sameness of mind in meditation, daily activities, dream and sleep, then we will also know that sameness during death.

So we can practice relating to dying in meditation by settling our mind in its own nature. Having done so, we can ask "Who am I?" Rather than thinking about answers, we can practice by looking directly at who we are. Discovering the unborn nature of mind, of experience, and of our identity, we become free from the conventional notions of who we are and of "death."

Still we are inclined to ask, so what happens to our continuum of consciousness? Will, for example, our consciousness transfer or be reabsorbed into to the "indestructible mind" and its five aspects? There are many who believe that a continuum of consciousness is possible, although clearly, we will not be taking all of our baggage along on the journey. The answer here is just as we have a continuum of consciousness from before birth to birth, from daily activities to deep sleep, from dream to dream, so we shall continue to "have it" from life to "after life."

This may seem somewhat disappointing, but if we treat life and death as being a matter of accumulating possessions, such as an identity and knowledge, and feel that we should work towards taking as much baggage along on the journey of death as possible, then we are wasting our time.

By cultivating awareness and virtue we will have all the baggage we need, and matters will take care of themselves.

We have had the experience of our human birth but most of us do not know how to remember our own birth from an experiential perspective. We can practice by investigating the continuum of our consciousness from moment to moment in the present. Then we can consider our consciousness five minutes ago, a day ago, a week ago, a year ago, back to our earliest childhood memories. We may feel we are the same person now, but we should question what it is that really is the same. What is the continuum of consciousness that we are so attached to?

Our investigation does not have to stop here. We can look at our consciousness before we learned to organize information through language and cognitive structures within our mind. Who were we then?

Just as we can return to our past, our roots, by directly investigating who we were, so we can pursue the same approach with regard to our future identities. Who will we be tomorrow, the next day, when ill, when healthy, when we die? Investigating the matter this way, we can travel through time to our death. Here again it is important not to imagine death as happening to us in the future but as something happening to us in the present, right here and now. We travel to the future but it is no longer "there"; rather it is right here. Again we should consider who we are that dies in the now. We can look directly at the answer to this question and so doing come face-to-face with the union of awareness and openness.

But what about the dear memories of our parents or our children or our friends in life. Naturally we do not want to forget these. Here we should ask ourselves what it is that we cling to about these people, these experiences. Is it their form? How is it when they cut their hair, or when the lighting happens to change, and their appearance changes? Is the form truly intrinsic to those to whom we are so attached? What about their smell, their feel, or their color? No, none of these are it either.

So if it is not their body, is it their personality, their character that endears us so? Is it their use of the language, or the kindness that they have manifested from time to time? Is it their delightful playfulness that endears us? We can ask whether this makes up who our loved one is or if there is something more.

Ultimately we will find that that which endeared someone else to us is no other than that which we value in life itself. We can and will miss a person's unique character and presence so much it will move us to tears. However, the reflections of waves do not exist as such, and even here it is evident that there is nothing to cling to.

Finally, we should look clearly at who is it that is doing the clinging? Who are we? How are we able to possess anything? Clearly in the dance of space and time, possession is a fiction, no one possesses anything. And eternal possession is like a fiction imposed upon a fiction.

This does not imply that in life we don't give our love completely to our companions. On the contrary, a deep love takes us directly into the timeless and vast qualities of mind itself. Rocking an infant to sleep in the middle of the night we are at peace and the universe is whole. There is nothing lacking. Holding our father's hand as he dies we are completely together in a timeless fashion.

Clinging to the form, which is our ingrained tendency, does not help matters at all. Eliminating our clinging also does not help matters at all. If we cling it is OK but the important point is not to add to this clinging anything extra. We do not need to become obsessed with clinging. If we cling, then just cling. If we do not cling, that is OK too. This is not a measure of our wisdom or greatness. It can just be our personality shining through.

When we die, if we should suffer, that is OK, that is our condition. But let us not compound the suffering. If when we die, we are ready to die and go peacefully, that is OK; that is our condition. There is nothing to get attached to here; no performance is required. And when we die we finally let go of the need to perform, to accomplish, to gain anything.

In dying, our old condition transforms itself into a new one. The freshness of our new condition, at first strange, may begin to feel quite familiar to us. Indeed, we may welcome this with awe.

If during life we have dwelled in conceptual existence, we will be troubled by conceptual existence at death. If we have been able to return to our vast mind and recognize it in all that transpires, we will find that the freedom of life, the self-liberation of life, will be no other than the self-liberation of death. We are completely ready for death, even if subject to a most traumatic death.

Bringing Illness to the Path

So how do we "bring illness to the path"?

When ill, we tend to worry about things. We may worry about our appearance or our ability to get around being impaired or if there will be some lasting consequences from our illness. We may worry about income for the family. We have to consider all of these things and come to terms with them on a personal level, straight-up and without adding too much extra anxiety. We should seek the doctors of our time for medical treatment, if required, and make intelligent, informed decisions regarding our health care in conjunction with medical experts. Of course anxiety will not help us and may even add to our illness, but addressing our illness intelligently can help us work towards a cure.

However, we can also relate to our illness in a more direct and immediate fashion. We can look at our illness directly. We should understand the nature of our illness as being no other than the nature of mind and we should understand this thoroughly.

This understanding doesn't necessarily end the illness. However, it will help us to find balance with respect to it and prevent some of the deeper suffering which would otherwise accompany it. It gives us a degree of freedom from our illness, and with that degree of freedom, we have the possibility of complete freedom.

More on Dying with Awareness

If our illness is terminal, once again we come face-to-face with our death. At some point it will not leave the room, no matter how much we wish or pray for it to do so. In this case, there is some simple advice for those close to death and for us to take to heart.

As in life, so in death, our mind will act as the basis, the path, and the fruit of our universe. In life, it is the one constant we have known, an indestructible union of openness and luminosity. Now, at this very moment, we should see that it is a union of openness and luminosity. When dying, regardless of what we experience, we will still have this open and clear nature. Whatever arises, right there in that condition is the clarity. Whatever arises, right there is the openness.

This openness, from our individual perspective, expresses itself as perpetual change. That is the compassion of its nature. And it is due to this dynamic and luminous nature that we may also become quite bewildered during the death process. As we die, our dynamic nature becomes extraordinarily self-evident and changes seem to take place at increasingly rapid rates; everything is out of control.

From the luminous clarity of our mind, projections arise. Indeed, the very clarity of our mind is what can act to confuse us. Just as very vivid pictures on the movie screen look real, so it is with all the projections of our mind. We may have experiences of light or deep grinding sounds or quite strong and unusual sensations.

Here it is important to look at whatever arises directly.

This is the advice we can give a loved one who is passing away. Whatever happens, look at it directly.

What is there to do as we die? "Just die, with mindfulness and caring" is the answer we can give; just as in living the key instruction can be condensed into "just live, with mindfulness and caring."

Living, sleeping, dreaming, dying, we maintain a presence of awareness. Through this we come to live in the mirror aspect of mind as well as its reflections.

Also when someone we know is dying or severely ill, we naturally feel great compassion for them and try to do what we can to help them. Here we can also acknowledge the nature of our mind, even in the midst of feeling pain for others. And even here we may come to the freedom of mind.

Life and death are not some training ground for us, like a gigantic battlefield with many obstacles. Rather the problem seems to be that we have become so habituated to restrictive ways of seeing and living, that our recognition of the diamond nature of mind, precious and indestructible, is almost completely obscured. It is precisely this diamond mind which provides the basis for both our confusion and liberation.

Eventually we come to a point where the clouds and obscurations themselves are nothing but an expression of our minds, the freedom of life itself. And in coming to know this, instead of finding ourselves in a battlefield, it is more as if we are in a world of self-perfection and self-liberation, like a great opera or rock concert where every participant performs his or her part to perfection.

And the universe is in awe.

Complete Confidence in Mind

Initially it is as if the universe is torn asunder,
But after a while, these excitements vanish
And we return to living simply and directly.

Free and at ease, we are completely content
As the one we are right now.

The Dawning of Certainty

Recognizing and addressing our doubts, again and again, looking at who we are, again and again, eventually we come to confidence.

Confidence is not arrogant or loud. It just keeps us going about our own business. And in the process all are benefitted.

No longer afraid of success or failure, we can do anything we wish with our life. We begin to feel that we do have endless choices and that we have the power to realize our goals and positively shape each and every environment we face. No more fears, no more hopes gnawing at us.

This does not mean that we don't fear for the safety of our children as they cross the street, or that we don't hope for good health and a good education for them, in addition to basic happiness and self-understanding. We still possess practical fears but may find ourselves to be completely without other fears.

During the Sixties there was a popular joke which played on a statement of a former president. "There is nothing to fear except fear itself, and of course the bogeyman!" After we get in touch with the nature of fear, these are exactly the fears which vanish. The unfounded fears, fear of fear itself and fears of fictitious causes and events of terror.

We no longer mistake the rope on the path for a snake. We can begin to see things clearly and in doing so the many snakes of our life vanish completely.

Hatred, jealousy, envy, arrogance, all of these negative emotions are then understood with greater clarity. When they arise, we can look right at what they are, and in doing so come to know that their nature is no other than the nature of mind itself. In this way, they are self-liberated and we diffuse their destructive aspects. We can take pride in our work without demeaning someone else. We can communicate our anger clearly to those who intend to harm us or our family, if this is required to ensure their protection, minimizing any destructive consequences or transforming them into positive consequences.

Bringing Sleep and Trauma to the Path

When we start out on the path of direct perception, of understanding mind, we may develop a preference for the clear and open awareness that we discover in everything we do. This awareness is a wonderful event in our lives. It is the start of realization of the wisdom of our lives. However, we will still encounter states of mind which we feel to be less attractive, such as deep sleep or the shock of unexpected trauma. We do not feel ready to acknowledge that deep sleep and trauma are also, in essence, the same as our more composed and reasonable selves.

For example, we may feel that we should some-how learn to remain awake all the time, thus avoiding the darkness of deep sleep. This aspiration indicates that we are not free of our attachment to certain states and aspects of mind over others. Having this view indicates that we still need to deepen our familiarity with the nature of our mind. In addition, it shows that we are clinging to simplistic ideas of self-existence and self-permanence. With this mistaken view, we may even develop a kind of arrogance because we regard it to be superior to require less sleep than others!

This clinging to certain states of mind can be quite evident as we go to sleep. A strong clinging to the bright and open awareness of our meditation indicates that we have not brought sleep to the path.

We must begin to realize mind and who we are right in the midst of sleep itself. Realizing this, we also will more naturally realize mind in trauma and death. This approach is a very skillful and gentle way of accomplishing an important stabilization of our recognition of the nature of mind.

How do we practice bringing sleep to the path?

As we go to sleep, we simply rest our mind in its natural state. Although initially we may just fall asleep, with time we may find that even the dark and impenetrable mind of sleep begins to take on a some-what more awake quality. We can have continuity of awareness through sleep. This takes place, not in a conventional sense, but rather via the continuity of mind essence, the union of luminosity and openness. This experience may be described as "pouring water into water." Sitting awareness pours into daily living, which in turn pours into sleep, which in turn flows into daily living. No difference in essence although they manifest differently. Even traumatic experiences can be included in this. Indeed traumatic experiences provide us with a unique opportunity to come closer to realizing the essence of mind, if we are ready. It is interesting to note that the root of the word trauma is "traum" which has the same meaning as dream.

At this point we may also let go of our obsessions with other experiences which may arise as a result of meditation practice. For example, it is not unusual for a meditator to become awake, with unusual clarity, within a dream. Once awake in a dream, he or she can exercise endless phenomenal powers in the dream realm. Within a dream one can fly through space, go through the earth, invite the presence of beings, and have extraordinarily profound or titillating meditative experiences. At this stage, however, the thrill of mastering the dream state is relaxed and the dream state becomes just a part of the overall confidence of mind.

Whatever our condition, whatever our manifestation, whatever our expression, we realize the freedom of mind.

Through this we can recognize even our ordinary mind to be free of birth, existence, and cessation. This ordinary mind is our greatest treasure. There is nothing that can be added to it or taken away from it. In our ordinary mind, nothing is lacking.

Here we no longer have to make an effort to maintain our mindfulness. If we feel disturbed about being distracted, then we ask "Who is disturbed, who goes astray?" and "To where do we go astray?" Once we realize, with certainty, that there is no going astray, our mindfulness remains constantly fresh.

And in coming to know this, we have achieved complete confidence in mind.

Self-Liberation of Our Ordinary Mind

Confusion and ignorance,
*   Wherever we may encounter them,*
In ourselves and others,
*   Become our path entirely.*

A Celebration of Life

Awakened mind is not the possession of a particular lineage of transmission or religion or sect. It is available to all of us at any time in our lives. Still it is helpful for us to pursue our investigation of ourselves in some challenging and comprehensive fashion. The problems of life are there to be probed.

When we have begun to trust in our mind, deeply, completely, we find that there is nothing left that we have to do. This does not cause us to become idle, but rather we find that this trust is accompanied by a self-perpetuated sense of kindness and alertness.

In the morning we get up and have breakfast. Then, walking briskly, we catch our bus and go off to work. In the evening, the baby cries and we get up to nurse her. As tired as we are, we change her diapers.

We do not concern ourselves with receiving recognition for our knowledge and accomplishments because that is not at all the issue here. We can completely trust in ourselves. We realize that we have a tremendous resource with us at all times, in every condition.

This trust or faith in mind exists so deeply that we do not feel inclined to fabricate spiritual paths for people to journey on. We realize that everyone has their own path and that their own innate wisdom is as great as our own.

Our respect for our fellow human beings reaches its height here and we can be with them whether it is at a barbecue, a common crisis, or a good poker game.

There is nothing to preach. We value our path to the utmost and can also help others progress on their paths effectively. This occurs not by replacing one belief system with another, or one value system with another, but by helping them to come back to the value of their lives.

This celebration of life becomes a reality for us. We can find intimacy with ourselves and with others, completely. We no longer add to the confusion. Confusion and ignorance, wherever we may encounter them, in ourselves and in others, become our path entirely.

Peaceful Coexistence

At some point
  Direct understanding of mind
Is completely present in our lives,
  Without effort or contrivance.

A Mind of Peace

It is wonderful to have a path which works for us and which can clearly establish the way for others, regardless of whether this way is called Advaita Vedanta or Buddhism or Christianity or Hinduism or Islam or Judaism or Taoism or Yoga. We may find the path of self-understanding through direct perception helpful and wish to share it with others.

Still, on the way of self-understanding through meditation we will come to what is called "non-meditation." Here we jump from the four concepts of "knowing self," "forgetting self," "both knowing self and not knowing self," and "neither knowing nor not knowing self" straight to unfabricated or unmodified being. Here there is no more meditator or act of meditation, no knower or act of knowing; the three spheres of subject, action, and object are released.

Here, it is said, we regard all as a display of awareness. We abandon our clinging to any contrived form of meditation or self-identity. We find our balance at all times and in all situations. And even this balance may or may not be apparent to others.

Ultimately, if we cling to our practice, we will not find complete peace, not for ourselves and not for others. This does not mean that we should at some point abandon our practice. Rather it means that at some point our direct understanding of mind is completely present in our lives, without any effort or contrivance.

We can gauge whether we require more sitting meditation practice by how caught up we are in conflicting emotions and conceptual worlds. If we are feeling as if we need to do more, then this is indeed the case. If we force our practice of sitting meditation so much that our mind becomes exceptionally wild or unsettled, then we should get up and walk around and work more on non-sitting practice. We can use our own judgement.

If we can live with mindfulness, vigilant awareness, and kindness in our lives, whatever our condition, we have brought forth the highest virtue of our lives. Realizing the depths of mind, our ordinary mind — free from elaboration, the sameness of appearances, thoughts, and mind, we have truly begun to live.

Simple and uncomplicated, we are at peace with whomever we are with, whatever we are doing. Even the waves and whirlpools of our mind are recognized to have an essence of peace.

Our sense of respect for others engenders a strong space of mutual respect. There is room and time for all of our idiosyncrasies. Everything has its place. Nothing plays a more important role than anything else. Whether we are the CEO or the mail clerk, teacher or student, it makes no difference at all.

Both purities are realized; the originally pure nature, which we have always had, and the freedom from our conflicting emotions and conceptual dualities, which we have cultivated based on our original purity.

No longer driven by the need to do something with our lives, we also find that our desires and wishes have not vanished. Instead the wish to do something of meaning with our lives can be realized in the fullest sense. We can aspire to do something of meaning precisely because the intrinsic meaning of everything is realized.

This is our human condition. Our thirst and cries can coexist peacefully with the depths of our existence. There is no contradiction here, not even a paradox; just a unity of luminosity and openness.

We continue to thirst for more although this thirst is quenched again and again. The complete perfection of everything "as it is," and the endless work towards our aspirations, within our condition, "as it appears," can coexist peacefully.

And regardless of its appearance, our life feels complete and intimate, just as it is...

In New York, running on the streets, my feet slap the hard concrete and cobblestone; in Ohio, playing blues by Mosquito Lake, the music brings laughter; in Vermont, the colors of autumn adorn Camel's Hump; in California, one child on my back, the other in hand, the dry air burns my nostrils; in Alaska, suddenly face-to-face with a moose; in Texas, corporate strategies and the heat cut to the core. These have been my condition.

Nowadays, in the fall, the moon comes up over Sonoma Mountain. In the morning, sometimes it is foggy, at other times the sky is a vivid blue.

❁

May all be happy, through and through!

❁   ❁   ❁

Appendix

Extra Meditation Practices

Practices for Appreciating Our Human Birth

Overall Description

The purpose of these practices is to awaken a deep appreciation of the preciousness of life and its time, space, awareness, ground, and continuity aspects.

Reflections of Time and Space

We can easily imagine a cubic inch of space, or a cubic foot, since these dimensions are common to our experience and thus easily visualized by our minds. Similarly, it is not too difficult to imagine the passage of five seconds of time or one minute.

In this practice, we work with our own measures of space and time.

Space

We begin by imagining a space circumscribed by an imaginary sphere one inch in diameter. When this is quite clear to us and seems familiar to us, we imagine, in turn, the following sequence of sizes:

- a space which is about one foot in diameter
- a space one mile in diameter
- a space one earth size in diameter
- a space one solar system in diameter
- a space as vast as the known limits of the universe
- a space which extends without limits

Spend anywhere from one to five minutes on each visualization. The sizes can be approximate in sense, and if it helps, can include imagined objects, such as the world or the planets of the solar system, to help establish them.

Really feel the relative sizes of these spaces. Feel as if your mind actually embraces spaces as large as imagined.

Now shift the focus back to a space an inch in diameter. In turn, imagine spaces of the following sizes:

- a space the size of a hard pea
- a space the size of the finest particle of sand
- a space the size of a cell in your body
- a space the size of an atom
- a space the size of a subatomic particle, like a proton
- an endlessly small space

Here it may be necessary to imagine "objects" in these spaces to enable one to imagine their sizes. We can explore these large or small spaces by moving through them in our imagination. We can be very playful about our investigations, making sure we capture the flavor of each size before moving on to another level.

Time

With regard to time, we begin by imagining the passage of a minute. Then in turn we imagine "time" of the following durations:

- a time on the order of one hour
- a time on the order of one day
- a time on the order of one year
- a time on the order of one thousand years
- a time on the order of one million years (a thousand times a thousand)
- endless time

Here imagined sets of events can help define the extent of time.

Similarly, we can imagine the following short times:

- a time on the order of a second
- a time on the order of a hundredth of a second
- a time on the order of a millionth of a second
- a time on the order of a millionth of a millionth (or trillionth) of a second
- an endlessly small moment of time

What should become apparent from these exercises in imagination is that the size of space is established by the size of the objects associated with that space; similarly the extent of time imagined is defined by the events which we associated with passage of time. Size of space and duration of time are meaningless when dealing with space and time themselves.

The Space and Time of Our Lives

Now imagine the space of our body relative to "all of space." Experience both the contrast and the sameness of these two measures of time. Similarly, imagine all of time relative to one life span. Again experience the contrast between these two spaces and also the elements of sameness between the imagined spaces. Is there a difference in quality between these two spaces and these two times or is there only a difference in quantity?

Now if our body and its life span seem very small compared to all of space and time, let us reflect on the space and time of our body relative to the "smallest possible" space and time. Suddenly "our space and time," when compared to the smallest space and time, appear as vast as the universe's space and time compared to "our own."

In some respects, our ordinary life is but a lightning flash in the sky while in other respects it endures as long as the sky itself.

These discoveries may also lead one to observe how relative any measures of space and time are. Imaginary space and time, as conceived of by our minds, are themselves presented by the play of our own awareness. Rather than dealing with time and space as projections of mind, we can relate to them as intrinsic aspects of our life itself, of the play of awareness itself.

First let us take a look at a practice which may help us understand certain aspects of our awareness which we may or may not have noticed before.

Reflections of Awareness

We begin by just relaxing in a stable but comfortable position. We relax body and mind, dropping them off, as if we no longer have to hold them up through our own efforts.

We know that we are alive. There is some quality to our experience which allows us to declare with complete confidence "I am alive." We can just relax and taste this aliveness for a little while.

Now we can ask "Who am I that sees all this, that knows all this?" Rather than endlessly repeating the question, we now look directly (with our mind) at the one who sees all this. In this way we may come to know the seeing or knowing quality of mind itself.

We may also observe that whenever we look for this seeing quality, it is there. And although we can say there is this seeing quality, we cannot say anything else about it. This seeing quality is the transcendent aspect of our awareness.

Similarly, our awareness may present itself in our thoughts, self-image, and an endless array of experiences.

Our awareness is both participatory in nature and transcendent.

Attending to the Five Aspects of Mind

Now we can consider the five elements of mind in a more direct fashion. These practices can be done while sitting in meditation or during any of life's activities where and when safety permits.

First we attend to the knowing quality of mind. We observe the knowingness of everything which arises with all of our experience. In some sense this knowingness is the same as the one we touch when we look for the seer of our experience; in other respects it is different, it may contain its own individual characteristics.

Second, we can attend to the space aspects of experience directly. All of our experience, even sound and feeling have spatial aspects to them. We can also attend to the space of awareness itself.

Third, we attend to the dynamic aspects of experience and awareness. The endless dynamism of experience has a definite timeless quality to it. Nothing can stop it. We can know this with certainty.

Fourth, we may attend to the ground from which all of our experience arises, mind itself. And finally, we may observe the continuity which we see in our lives, both in the conventional sense of how we can recall past events and in a unconventional sense of continuity of these aspects within and beyond our own personal continuum.

We can spend weeks just attending to one particular aspect, if we wish. By being mindful of these various aspects of our experience we may find that our thirst and demand for particular events in our life begin to diminish. We no longer feel pressured to collect time or experiences or knowledge as commodities which will satisfy us. Instead we discover that we have an endless, vast resource of time and space and awareness at our constant disposal. We can appreciate everything which arises, even this very moment.

Addendum

If you have questions or comments about your experience with practices in *Piercing the Autumn Sky* or are interested in receiving information about related workshops or retreats, please write to:

Mahamudra Meditation Center
P.O. Box 750681-P
Petaluma, CA 94975-0681
USA.

Mahamudra Meditation Center is a non-profit, religious corporation founded to facilitate the instruction, study, and practice of this path of awareness and kindness.